ALSO BY JUNE JORDAN

LIBRETTO AND LYRICS BY

june jordan

MUSIC COMPOSED BY

john adams

ORIGINAL PRODUCTION DIRECTED BY

peter sellars

SCRIBNER

New York • London • Toronto • Sydney • Tokyo • Singapore

I Was Looking at the Ceiling and Then I Saw the Sky

earthquake/romance

SCRIBNER
1230 Avenue of the Americas
New York, NY 10020

Designed by Jennifer Dossin

Manufactured in the United States of America
3 5 7 9 10 8 6 4 2

Library of Congress Cataloging-in-Publication Data is available.

ISBN 0-684-80422-0

for the one
who
standing in the sun
does not cast a shadow

acknowledgments

Big thanks to John Adams and Peter Sellars.

Thanks to my agent, Frances Goldin, who, tenacious and loving, fought for the public birth of these words.

Thanks to my editor, Leigh Haber, whose delight and whose determination made it happen.

Thanks to Adrienne B. B. Torf, forever daring me to go ahead and try.

Thanks to David Dante Troutt, whose hilarity and eloquence kept me on track.

Thanks to Stephanie Rose, who volunteered to get married, onstage, every single opening night.

———

I wish to thank all the community activists and attorneys who gave me invaluable time and counsel on issues of criminal and immigration law, especially Margaret Lin, David Troutt, Sandra Gutierrez, Deanna Jang, Bill Hing, Bernita Reagan, Michael Friedman, and Van Jones.

Grateful acknowledgment to the co-commissioners: Cal Performances, The Regents of the University of California, Berkeley; Lincoln Center for the Performing Arts, Inc.; Thalia Theater in Germany; Bobigny Theater in France.

special acknowledgment

It is Peter Sellars who brainstormed all the way from the beginning with me. It is Peter Sellars who flew up from L.A., and who listened on the phone, and who called from Salzburg/New York/Chicago. It is Peter Sellars whose laughter and whose flights of delight and whose ecstatic response became my steady motivation and reward. I thank him, here, with my love.

I Was Looking
at the Ceiling and Then
I Saw the Sky

earthquake/romance

A contemporary romance carried by seven young men
and women living on the West Coast of the United States
in the nineties. For them, it's earthquake/romance:

It's like suddenly
It's like all that's going on
It's like very brief and underneath and on top
    of everything
It's like you never do get over it

the cast

All the characters are twenty-five years old or younger:

DAVID   A Black Baptist minister

LEILA   A Black graduate student working as a family planning counselor in an abortion clinic

CONSUELO   An undocumented immigrant mother of two, from El Salvador

MIKE   A White cop who is also a community activist

DEWAIN   A Black reformed gang leader

TIFFANY   A White TV crime-as-news reporter

RICK   A Vietnamese American Legal Aid defense attorney

a note about staging

The action of this opera takes place, mid-1990s, in Los Angeles.

I have left all other specifics to the discretion of the director.

But I have visualized this work within Elizabethan and/or Brechtian traditions of stagecraft.

contents
for act one and act two

ACT ONE

act

one

I Was Looking at the Ceiling and Then I Saw the Sky

CONSUELO

I thought everything was over and I had lost my
    lover
I thought my life was permanently out of order
because my world lay on the wrong side of some
    arbitrary border

DEWAIN

I thought that love and all the freedom of the
    air
would only last awhile before they had to disappear
I thought that I was preordained to fail
    and that
I'd never manage to stay out of jail

RICK

I thought she'd never give me anything much
but still I was dreaming about the weight
and the temperature
of her possible touch

LEILA

I thought he would never settle down
from chasing women all over town

DAVID

I thought I'd end up old and lonely because
one or another female wanted to become my one
and only

TIFFANY

I thought there was something
the matter with me
something only I couldn't see

MIKE

I thought love was strictly extracurricular
to what's important!
And that sex
in general
is not particular!

TUTTI

I was looking at the ceiling and then I saw the
    sky!
I was miserable and aching
at the way the news kept breaking
I was looking at the ceiling and then I saw the
    sky!
I felt broken into compromise
with nothing left to hope or prize
I was looking at the ceiling and then I saw the
    sky!
I was searching for a reasonable reason for my
    smile

I was finding what I want washed out completely
    in denial
I was looking at the ceiling and then I saw the
    sky!
I was looking at the ceiling and then I saw the
    sky!

CONSUELO
I thought that I would never find my place
where I could live without hiding my language
    and my face

DEWAIN
I thought happiness is like the laughter of a
    fool
And I was happy!

RICK
I felt like I was treading water
in between this country and Vietnam
I thought I'd never find my way
to someone who would give a damn

LEILA
I knew enough to know I didn't know
what happens when your heart
takes over and you have to
just let go

DAVID
I swore I'd end up old and lonely because
one or another female wanted to become my one
    and only

TIFFANY
I thought there must be something
the matter with me
something only I couldn't see

MIKE
I thought as long as I'm solid
and honest and strong
I don't have to worry about what if I'm wrong
     unless all along
I've got it all wrong!

TUTTI
I was looking at the ceiling and then I saw the
     sky!
I was miserable and aching
at the way the news kept breaking
I was looking at the ceiling and then I saw the
     sky!
I felt broken into compromise
with nothing left to hope or prize
I was looking at the ceiling and then I saw the
     sky!
I was searching for a reasonable reason for my
     smile
I was finding what I want washed out completely
     in denial
I was looking at the ceiling and then I saw the
     sky!
I was looking at the ceiling and then I saw the
     sky!

David spins out of the whole group and takes the stage. He delivers his Black Baptist Sermon of Romance dedicated to Leila.

David's Solo
(with Leila's Counterpoint)

DAVID

Let me tell you the Gospel
According to This Girl
Like to make me
Lose my Religion
(Hallelujah!)
Make me
tremble
(Lord God Almighty!)
Make me
shiver
(Good Father)
Make me
make me
feel the spirit
(Sweet Sweet Jesus)
Make me
make me
make me
slap my hands
Make me

make me
move my feet
and beg and beg for mercy!
Mercy!
Make me
make me
praise her name
Make me forsake
all other names
Tear up the pages
Forswear the numbers
Close my eyes
and concentrate
(devoted)
concentrate
I can't wait
I can't wait
to see this girl
again
this Serious Child of God
this Stunning Holy Sister
this Paragon of Personality
and Face and Form
beyond description
beyond the willing worship
of my open arms
Oh!
Oh!
I can't wait
I concentrate
I feel the spirit
overtake my sinner's body
overtake my sinner's body
feels the spirit

(Hallelujah!)
Makes me tremble
(Lord God Almighty!)
Makes me
shiver
(Good Father)
Makes me
makes me
feel the spirit
Glory
Glory
Glory

LEILA'S COUNTERPOINT

Glory
Gloria/Aisha/Rosalind/Patricia
which
little girl you screaming for?
the one you took home
yesterday
the one you met
this afternoon
the one you talk to when
I'm not around?
(and God knows how many more?)
(Holy/Hallelujah/Hey!
She's gone
so I can play?!)
Gloria/Aisha/Rosalind/
Patricia
which
little girl you screaming for?

A family planning office inside an abortion clinic. Leila works here, part-time, and Consuelo is seeking contraceptive advice.

Leila's Song of the Wise Young Woman

(with interjections from Consuelo)

LEILA

(Girl) I can't believe you're asking these
  questions!
What is the matter with you?
I'm glad you've come back to the clinic
but how can I get you to use some protection?
What do I have to do?

CONSUELO

But what of my heart!
I love my babies!
my six-year-old son of El Salvador!
my seven-month-old *hija de* Los Angeles!

LEILA

If he's the kind of a brother with fifteen women
  on his mind
You better get yourself another
  man

Don't be a sucker!
Don't step into some Big Mac Plan!

CONSUELO

But I never have to worry
Whenever we're apart!
Each of my children comes from
Something that I believe in
and a lover I never want to forget!

LEILA

Beat this message into your head
And lay down this baseline deep on drums
We gotta use condoms condoms condoms
Or go to the movies instead!

CONSUELO

Pero
what is more beautiful than the babies
born of a lust
for justice and dignity
—and me?!
I know you think I am Not so very smart
And my English it is not good
But each time we kiss and we start
to be close together and I am asking him whether
or not he thinks that we should—

LEILA

I don't care how cute he is
I don't care how fine
if you can't be his
one and only
You need to move on down the line

CONSUELO

But who are you
talking about? It is not me!
That is not my difficulty!
My problem is when am I able
to buy or find food I can put on the table!

LEILA

How many babies you planning to raise
by yourself
in Spanish or English and God knows What?
Don't you think two is more than enough
when babies and boyfriends is all
That you've got?

Girlfriend! I am no Angel and I'm not the Pope
but I'm not steering you wrong!
You better get with it! The Rope
for hanging yourself up is not (Really)(very) long!

And as for me
well, as for me
I tell you the little I know!
Sex is great but
It's not the same as public education!
I mean it's not what my momma would call an
        upwardly mo-bile pre-occupation!
It's not the end
of anything!

It's more like something you send
on one wing
hoping
the two of you will fly

someplace amazing and then
lie down but then get up
together

Hey! I am no Angel and I'm not the Pope
but I'm not steering you wrong!
You better get with it! The Rope
for hanging yourself up is not (Really)(very) long!

Dewain on the sunshine streets outside the Church.

Dewain's First Solo

DEWAIN

I got sunlight
on the doorknob
I got sunlight
on my key
I got sunlight
in my pocket
I got light all over me

I got sunlight
through the window
I got sunlight
on my shoes
I got sunlight
on my blues
I got light all over me

Where am I now and where will I go?
How do I figure out what I should know?
Slammin' the streets or slammin' for school
I'm fixin for tricks (said) I'm ready for treats
whatever the mix
Where am I now and where will I go?
How do I figure out what I should know?

I got sunlight
on the table
I got sunlight
on my chair
I got sunlight
and it's network and it's cable
I got sunlight
in my hair
I got sunlight
and I'm free!
I got sunlight
I got light all over me

Consuelo in her kitchen.

¿Dónde Estás?

CONSUELO

My Son!
It is so Late!
Have the Soldiers
captured you too!

El Salvador/Los Angeles
No hay diferencia
el secuestro la tortura
la falta del refugio
¿Dónde estás?
¿Dónde está mi hijo? *

¡Es tan tarde!
¿Te han capturado
los Soldados?

El Salvador/Los Angeles
What is the difference to me?
The death squads that murdered your father
the INS hunting us down!
And I must not open my mouth!
We live in secret
We live in silence from North
to South/Oh!

There is no safety
in any village any city any town/No!
Not for us!/Oh!
My son!
¡Es tan tarde!
¿Te han capturado?

*(What is the difference to me?
The Kidnap the Torture
The No Place to Run
Where are You/
Where is my Son?)

Mike and David inside a great big Baptist church where David works as the young, fast-rising, new, activist Baptist minister, and Mike heads up several youth programs.

Song about a Man among Men and a Man among Many Women

MIKE

It's a really cool feeling to deal like a man among
    men
The police corps, the Army, and basketball at night!
It gives me a whole lotta pride that I must be doing
    (something) right!

DAVID

For me it's a different kind of thing
because it's the ladies who carry the Church
and I love all those females under my wing!

MIKE

I'm lucky to move like a man among men
It gives me a way to work with the guys
I yank them outta gangs and drug stuff and then
it's counseling for jobs if my strategy flies

DAVID

For me it's a different kind of thing

I lead as I please; I have privilege divine
and the Church and the women make sure that I shine
But me and my women—

MIKE

But me and my men—
Still we collaborate

DAVID

(More or less, yes!)

MIKE

And we do pretty good on the street

DAVID

(Well, hell, we'd better, I guess!)

MIKE

There's so much to keep going!

DAVID

Workshops in math
and prenatal care
Heritage Studies
and food for the homeless
AIDS counseling
and senior
and young-adult choirs
The Street Band for Christ
and Little League flyers!
Anything to make the community strong!

MIKE

Anything so we straighten things out and we keep things
     clear

So we all know (like) exactly who we are
and nobody's confused or demoralized or queer!
I'm not about to teach baseball to queers!

DAVID
Anything to keep the Honeys buzzing in the hive
full of delectable sweets and between-meal treats
with cookies and bake sales and coffee cake and chicken
and so many questions! And so many answers!
And Birthday clubs and socials and dances
    and some of those delightful lovely
    lovely dancers!

MIKE
I tell them: show me that you know what it takes to
    be a man!
Square those shoulders!
Tuck that butt!
Suck in that gut!
Lift that chin!
What's supposed to happen when you get older
if you don't train now like you really mean to win!
Be proud! Be a man!
And make sure the whole world knows it:
Here comes a man and his walk and his talk: Everything
    shows it!
Don't slouch like a coward or mince like a fag!
Build your body! Stay clean! Hang tough! And your
    manhood's in the bag!

DAVID
For me it's a very different kind of thing!

MIKE
I'm lucky to move like a man among men!
And still we collaborate!

DAVID
(More or less, yes!)

MIKE
And we do pretty good on the street!

DAVID
(Well, hell, we'd better, I guess!)

Elsewhere onstage:
We see Dewain in a phone booth, taking the call from
Consuelo (her solo "¿Dónde estás?"). As she concludes,
we see Dewain hang up the telephone and try to decide
what he needs to do before beginning his emergency run to
rescue Consuelo. We see him stop to pick up two bottles of
beer from a local convenience store. There is a long line at
the checkout and he doesn't wait around to pay.
   As he leaves the store, we see Mike arrest him, and
Tiffany recording the whole episode on camera.

Mike explains the arrest procedure to Tiffany.

Mike's Song about Arresting a Particular Individual

MIKE
Spread your legs!
Both hands on the car!
(I'm following a regular procedure
this way he can't try any funny stuff
And he damn straight can't go far!)
Down on your knees!
Cross your hands behind your back!
(This way he can't try to impede your
arrest procedure and by adding on this handcuff
thing it makes him more or less freeze
While his public immobility cuts me some slack!)
You have the Right to remain Silent!
(I'm telling him his Rights!
This individual is one of our local community Lights!
A real gang-banger! A Leader of Thugs!
Everyone around here knows his stupid mug
and they listen to him and they trust
This joker! So you have to be careful
how you bust
him/This alleged criminal

Out on the Streets!
He'll get a high-price attorney to broker
a Second and Third gift of probation
for good behavior/his alleged reform
That's the norm!
And then on the next day the next punk perpetration
of another felonious violation
will implicate
him
again!
This particular individual
I know very well!
Hell! I honestly believed that this one
had really turned around!)
            Keep your eyes on the ground!
            Don't move!

Everyone but Tiffany recedes from front and center stage.
She sings about her wonderment and Mike.

Tiffany's Solo

TIFFANY

How Far Can I Go in a Car
(Driven by a Cop)
How far can I go
before the killer chill
of our intimate
situation
before the thrust and thrill
of our intimate
investigation
into murder/burglary/false
alarm/drug busts and
domestic altercations
overcome our actual
easy palpitations/overcome
the actual (and) natural charm
of riding
(side by side)
riding
in a car
(Driven by a Cop)
How far can I go?

How many ways do I
have to try
Before I succeed and get next
to this guy?

I'm trailing my hand on his thigh
I'm tickling my nails all over his knee

But whether it's homicide/mayhem or me
I'm not sure why he's hot or why he stays high!

We look like
We look like
a hellified couple
out
hunting down trouble

Oh God!
He's so fine! He's so strong!
I'm excited just tagging along!

It's so sweet!
Night after night in the car/night after night
on the passenger seat
I feel good I feel right
around and beside his beautiful head and his chest
and his beautiful legs and his beautiful feet

How many days do I
have to try
Before I succeed and get next
to this guy?

It's even okay if I fall asleep
because he's in charge/he's
a guy who can keep
things under control
no matter the roll
of the dice
He's eager! He's amazing! And
totally nice!

And still he's the one man I don't understand!

How far/Oh!

How far can I go in a car
(Driven by a Cop)?

Song about the On-Site Altercation

DEWAIN

I'm not your jungle bunny for the news!
Get that camera out of my face!

TIFFANY

I captured the whole thing on film! And besides
I saw you for myself!

DEWAIN

What's that supposed to mean?

TIFFANY

I saw you take those bottles off the shelf!

LEILA

Big Deal! Who's looking for clues?
That's nothing the Brother was trying to hide!

TIFFANY

But he didn't—(pay!)

LEILA

So what? It's not
A Big Deal!

MIKE

It's a criminal offense—

LEILA

Screw you and your girlfriend!

MIKE

Let's keep things calm! And clean! And clear!
Be careful or
I'm gonna have to book you too!

LEILA

Don't even try it! You better get real!
You're violating
my neighborhood/my space!

MIKE

As the arresting police officer on duty at this
      time
I must advise you
That it would probably be in your best
interests
to stop escalating
things!
Otherwise
I might have to amend
my report and change this from a misdemeanor
to a felony crime!

DEWAIN

A felony!

MIKE

You just tried to intimidate a witness!

DEWAIN
This is really really messed
up!

MIKE
It's on you Big Boy! If you cooperate—

DEWAIN
Take off these handcuffs/call me "boy" again
and I'll cooperate my fist upside your head!

TIFFANY
That's beautiful! That's precisely what
all of America wants to see!
Single-handedly
you'll make my ratings soar!
—Threatening an officer!

LEILA
Hey, I'm about to do more
than threaten the two of you bozos!
Why don't you shoot me?
Go ahead! Shoot!
What are you waiting for?
Don't try to act like you're
not hot
and bothered about
any excuse to take me out!
Shoot!

MIKE
I'm warning you!
Act right! Be polite
now

or I'll have to run you in
for incitement
to riot!

LEILA

Fine! I'll be quiet!
But you better believe you'll be
hearing from me
and the rest of us! A felony?!
No!
I don't think so!

*The three young women extricate themselves from their
various, but intersecting, situations and join together in a
song celebrating the existence of men on the planet.*

Song about the Bad Boys and the News

(trio by Leila, Consuelo, and Tiffany)

LEILA, CONSUELO, AND TIFFANY
For days I been dreaming about changing the news
For days I been dreaming about changing the news
but sometimes the news ain' something you choose

My mind is a camera and my body's a clock
(I say) my mind's like a camera and my body's a clock
But feelings invade me and leave me in shock

Political nightmare all over the place
I'm running relentless a circular race
And sometimes it scares me to see my own face

But then there's the bad boys
But then there's the bad boys
And when there's the bad boys
bad news can't do nothin' bad to me!

I'm talking about a seven-day kiss

I'm talking about *mucho* premarital bliss
I'm stalking down a seven-day kiss

I'm looking at his legs, honey! His
I-run-ten-miles-four-times-a-week-just-to-keep-my-
perspective legs! His
Legs!

He Run like a God
He do more'n That
like a God
like a do-Right-dude-in-the-all-night-delicatessen-
of-my-MTV-excitable excitement
he Run-Run-Run-Run-Run like a God!

Then there's his shoulders and then there's his smile
Then there's his voice and then there's my smile
Then there's the curly hair right below his belly button

Wait!/What about the buns!
Tight and High like African Suns!
(Get it, girl)
Like significant African Suns
and you notice them hot
and ripening between your
hands/your Thighs
(All Right, now!)

And then there's The Absolute Sleeper
The flower
The fish
and the bone
and the bone on the throne
and the delicate flesh on the bone

on the Throne
The pen on the pillow of sperm
The penis stretched out for Venus
The Thunderbolt
long as it's firm!

Oh! For days I been dreaming about changin' the news
My mind is a camera (and) my body's a clock
Political nightmare all over the Place

But then there's the bad boys
But then there's the bad boys
And when there's the bad boys
bad news can't do nothin' bad to me!

Elsewhere onstage:
We see Dewain, outside the courtroom, taken away into custody.

Your Honor My Client He's a Young Black Man

(Rick's solo)

RICK

Your Honor my Client He's a Young Black man
Your Honor my Client He's Not Really Impossible
    to Understand
So I ask you to try
Just as I/Just as I
Have to trust what I know/where I stand
in relationship to
This remarkable Black man!
He's enjoying the day on the street
He's heading in no particular direction
He's following the drift of his feet
But his beeper goes off
His girlfriend's number comes up
And because he hopes (of course) to keep her
this girlfriend the mother of his first and only child
a seven-month-old
a baby daughter he's wild
to protect and to hold
my Client is not inclined to delay or to scoff
at this sudden alarm

So he does what he believes
a Black man oughta do
He calls this young lady to inquire/to make
      sure that no harm
has befallen her out of the blue
Your Honor my Client He's a Young Black man
Your Honor my Client He's Not Really Impossible
      to Understand
He's just this minute back from a second term in jail
for a couple of wobblers with little or no reason
except that this man's a natural-born leader
and as you probably know it's always open season
on a Young Black man set up to fail!
I apologize if I digress
To get back to the point:
My Client/He's recently released. I guess
you could say he's just back from the joint
and his girlfriend/well, clearly he needs her!
She's waited for him and She wants him Right now!
Over the phone She tells him She can't find her son!
Immigration has taken him somewhere as bait!
She's screaming and crying! She's completely undone!
Maybe she should hide! Maybe he should
      bring her a gun!
What if they come to the house for the baby girl too!
Your Honor my Client He's a Young Black man!
He's familiar with the terror of the armies of the State
He will do/he will do
Whatever he must whatever he can
And he doesn't know why and he doesn't know how
But he'll Rush to his girlfriend and chill out her fears
He'll rescue her boy and Stop all her tears
He's Racing to stand there in front of her face—

Now here is where
(I would say) it's a cultural thing:
Momentarily
My Client strays from the path on his way:
(*Spoken*) He Snatches two bottles of beer
(*Sung*) One for his girlfriend and another one he figures
will help him to calm
Things down but then there's a crowd and he can't
    wait around just to pay
for two bottles of beer
Two cold forties from a local convenience store/Okay:
He steals them: Four Dollars and Thirty-nine Cents'
    worth of ice-cold brew
He's Thinking this has been a hella day
    for him and his girlfriend and two
    bottles of beer is not more than he's due!

Your Honor my Client He's a Young Black man
Your Honor my Client He's Not Really Impossible
    to Understand
They've stolen a Child! He's taken two beers!
Three strikes and he's facing forty-five years!

And one witness claims that my Client/
Allegedly he
(almost) took away her breath/But!
There was no injury!
There is no death!
Who has he hurt?
And what will we lose
if the law rules
inert
(which is what you may choose)

Your Honor my Client He's a Young Black man
Your Honor my Client He's Not Really Impossible to
     Understand
(I think) it's a Cultural Thing
His rage and his petty mistake!
Two bottles of beer and his life's now at stake!
I give you five dollars to cover the brew/it's a bargain!
For five bucks/for five bucks the Court
Can be through
with my Client or
if all of us lose we spend twenty-five *Thousand*
     a year
for the rest of his time incarcerated for
two bottles of beer!

Still inside the courtroom.

Dewain's Obbligato/Counterpoint to Rick's First Solo

DEWAIN

I messed up again!
I'm failing Consuelo!
The court won't allow me to speak!
I'm supposed to be vicious
but humble
and weak!

Go, Rick!
But you're wasting your time!
Two bottles of beer?
That's not the crime!

I am the criminal!
Check out my skin!
Talk all you want
but
I just can't win!

I messed up again
I'm failing Consuelo

The court won't allow me to speak!
I'm supposed to be vicious
but humble
and weak!

Consuelo in her kitchen.

Consuelo's Dream

CONSUELO

Refrain
I heard the Knocking at the door
I thought it might be the soldiers
But oh! My Love!
It was you forever
Coming back for more!

Night stars danced around our fears
The sirens never made a sound
And jasmine bloomed and perfumed the air
And peaches and cherries covered the ground

The baby lay sleeping and safe on the grass
And neighbors came by just to see
And my son was whispering (the names of) the things
        that you pass
on your way to a school where the teachers
        speak Spanish like me

And you *mi amor!* You gave me your lips
And you held me so close in the dark
That all of the violence fell into eclipse
And wasteland became like a wonderful park

And the earth began to rumble and roar
and buildings began to crumble and fall
And there was no house and (there was) no highway
    anymore
But you came to me suddenly serious and tall

And we stayed together forever and ever
And the enemies left us alone
And peaceful we lived on the banks of a river
More lovely than any the world's ever known

And you my beloved became A Rich Man
And I became as fat as my mother
And our baby became a beautiful woman
who adored and defended her very big brother

Refrain
I heard the Knocking at the door
I thought it might be the soldiers
But oh! My Love!
It was you forever
Coming back for more!

In the courtroom, Rick cross-examines Mike and Tiffany.

Rick's Cross-Examination of Tiffany and Mike

RICK

How do you two know each other?

MIKE

She has her job and I have mine.

RICK

No crossing the borders? No
fudging of boundaries?

MIKE

I do my job. She does her job.
It works out just fine.

RICK

No social dimension to your interaction?

MIKE

I do what I do. She sees what she sees!

RICK

For purposes of pure professional satisfaction
the two of you ride together side by side—

MIKE
Hey, nobody's lied
to you!

RICK
Then it's true?

MIKE
What?!

RICK
The two of you willingly submit to unusual
proximity—

MIKE
I don't follow you! This is insane!

RICK
—inside a small space
day after day
and still you say
there is "no social dimension"?
Next witness!

TIFFANY
Yes! I swear to tell the truth!

RICK
How do you two know each other?

TIFFANY
Professional necessities!

RICK

He is not your boyfriend or your brother?

TIFFANY

Right! And I am not your girlfriend
or your mother!

RICK

For purposes of pure professional satisfaction
the two of you ride together side by side—

TIFFANY

It's just exactly like whatever he said!
Obviously, we've got nothing
to hide!

RICK

The two of you willingly submit to unusual
prolonged
and intimate
physical proximity—

TIFFANY

What kind of a birdbrain—

RICK

—inside a small physical space hour
after hour and day after day
and still you say
there is "no social dimension"?

TIFFANY

I find this line of questioning and suggestioning
impertinent and inane!

RICK

Is there a failure of attention?
Would it be abnormal and unnatural
for a friendship to develop?
And would it be abnormal and unnatural
for Romance to deepen and enhance
for Romance to deepen and envelop
your mutual comprehension?

TIFFANY

Wait a second—

RICK

And since the two of you solemnly swear to improbable
assertions
such as No
Social Dimension
to your daily exertions
would it be abnormal and unnatural
for the two of you
to join in cruel collusion
at the expense of my client
jeopardized by the intrusion
of (very) (personal) loyalties
aided and abetted by your passionate attachment
as well?!

MIKE

Go to hell!

TIFFANY

Why don't you get back on a boat!

RICK

What do you know about me
or my family!
Two years searching for an open shore
or beach or anywhere
the fishermen could reach
—Thailand/Hong Kong/Singapore—
sometimes three hundred folk choked
together
on a miserable fishing boat
barely afloat
on the notion of America!

TIFFANY

Give me a break!

RICK

At least my father got permission
to come here!
Not like yours!

TIFFANY

Is it a cultural thing/these
people's children/They wash up on our shores
and then they
attack—

RICK

My family/we
are not some species
of fish!
And you do not look
like anybody's Native
American so

you have no
Right—

                    TIFFANY
Because I'm white? Oh,
please! This dis
would make (possibly) good
dialogue
for a news special
Sometime
But save it
Mr. Asian America—
I gotta go!

Rick stares at Tiffany and then, with no warning, he slips into this solo.

Rick's Awkward Love Song

RICK

I was thinking/actually
I wanted to/what
about lunch?
I wanted to/what
about last thing when
you close your/If
you think we could/I
would meet you there!/Well
I mean I wanted to/If
you/But
Since we met
I haven't been able to/which
I realize
maybe sounds like I want to forget
about (this is not working out!) If
You/Well
Okay! I wanted to/Actually
I was Thinking/What
about Lunch?

David visiting Dewain in jail.

Song about Law School as the Natural Follow-up to Jail

(duet by David and Dewain)

DEWAIN
De Reverend Doctor Feelgood I presume!

DAVID
Don't start!
Don't get smart!
We've raised the money for your appeal!
And I assume
that means a fifty-fifty chance to get
your Black butt back
and rolling
on that happy wheel
of ghetto roulette!

That woman/the witness
she may refuse to testify!
Because she's been listening to
her very special guy/the cop!
And he's a little bit sweet on Blackfolks!

DEWAIN

Oh yeah!
That's obvious!

DAVID

Hey! Sweet comes in different flavors!
Different strokes!
But remember
when you qualified
as his Absolute Pet Project
for interior and exterior
rehabilitation?

DEWAIN

Don't remind me!

DAVID

But he/But if you fry
it doesn't put him in the public eye
looking too much like a do-good hero!
And he wants that and he wants every one of you—

DEWAIN

One of who?

DAVID

. . . every one of you retarded/recidivist/and
irredeemable—

DEWAIN

Listen, Homeboy!
I can come straight through this bulletproof glass
and tighten up your ass!

DAVID

You always did
have a way with words!

DEWAIN

Better that I play with words
than women!
Your respectability
depends
on your detectability!
If you don't get caught
you're an okay Brother/But!
If anybody knew
how much you dog
around
you'd be through!
(That would) nail your philandering
flat feet
to the ground!

DAVID

You're just so basic
            homegrown
            doofus
            knock-kneed
            raggedy
            and dumb/
d-u-m-b
that you stopped to take two beers—

DEWAIN

I thought she might be thirsty!

DAVID

That's how come I gotta
call you
d-u-m-b dumb!

DEWAIN

Go
find yourself some ugly Babe in a tight
black dress
and lighten up!

DAVID

I tell you what!
You really need to get rid of that earring that
you been wearing!
That would help a lot!

DEWAIN

I'm planning to clean up my act!
I'll even wash windows!

DAVID

I'm talking about your salvation
and you like to act the fool!

DEWAIN

I'm serious!
I been thinking about Law School
as the natural follow-up
to jail!

If there's something that can get me in here
and then that something
can get me outta here

I figure
I should get into that something
and see what I can get out of it!

(DAVID

Yeah, sure!
"Law School as the Natural Follow-up
to Jail!")

Leila inside the abortion clinic.

Leila's Song:
Alone (Again or at Last)

LEILA

After all is said and done
I want to be somebody's straight-up Number One
After every crisis every problem like the setting of the sun
I want/somebody hold me close and tell me stories
     when it rains
I need/somebody break apart
       the meaning of the chains
       that choke my heart
After all is said and done
I want to be the reason for the sunrise and
     the flowers out of season
I want to be
I need to be somebody's
       dressed up
       dressed down
       naked
       three hundred sixty-five nights of one light
       year's piercing
       us tight
       together
       tight

     tight
     1 x 1
After all is said and done
I need to be
I want to be somebody's straight-up Number One!

The four young men extricate themselves from their various, but intersecting, situations and join in a song celebrating the existence of women on the planet. (Elsewhere onstage: We see Leila delivering a big pile of law-school textbooks to Dewain in his prison cell.)

Song about the Sweet Majority Population of the World

(Rick, Dewain, David, Mike)

TUTTI

Oooh!
The Sweet
Majority
Population
Of the World

Oooh!
Oh!
The Sweet
The Sweet
Majority
Ah!
The Sweet
Majority

Uuumph!
The Sweet Majority
Population
of the World

VARIOUS COMBINATIONS TAKING TURNS
Uuumph!
Oooh!
Oh!
Ah!
Uuumph!
Uuumph!
Oooh!

VARIOUSLY INTERMITTENT SOLOS

DEWAIN

That incredible
That lovely
Fifty-one percent
To me seems
like no accident

MIKE

That puzzlement
That mystery
To me seems
like love's history

DAVID

That agitation
That ultimate palpitation

– – – –

– – That infinite itch

RICK

That – – – –
That – – – –
Seems to me
like – – – –
I dunno!

TUTTI

The Sweet
Majority
Population
Of the World

act

TWO

David and Leila making out on the couch in David's office inside the Church.

Three Weeks and Still I'm Outta My Mind

(duet by David and Leila)

DAVID
Three weeks and still I'm outta my mind about you

LEILA
Three weeks and still I'm
    Thinking about you

DAVID
Three weeks and still I walk around blind without you

LEILA
Three weeks and still I'm
    watching what you do

DAVID
Don't send me no dead-end no Sorry
We're Through!
    I gotta get a program
    Compatible with you
I gotta get my disc to match your drive!

LEILA

How do you expect my heart to behave
unless you enter my love then *save*

DAVID

Three weeks and here I am still I can't stop
I'm crazy to see you! I'm ready to pop!
I wanna be the one you call to figure out the VCR

LEILA

I want you as the designated driver of my car

DAVID AND LEILA

What do I have to prove
to put my lovin' in the middle of your very next move?

LEILA

I'm trying not to come on too antagonistic

DAVID AND LEILA

But the Thought of my Losing you—

DAVID

I go ballistic!
If I
can't fly myself into the total energy
of your cyberkinetic
(you know)
astrophysiological configuration
If I can't fix myself
inside the anti-entropic
centripetal
space of your blow-me-away
hot

body's agile consummation
Baby
I'll just
I'll just have to think about
Somebody else!

                          LEILA
You said it! I heard you!
I'm outta here now!

                          DAVID
Baby here I am! Here I am still I can't stop!
Three weeks and still I'm outta my mind about you

                          LEILA
Three weeks and still I'm
    Thinking about you

                          DAVID
Three weeks and still I walk around blind without you

                          LEILA
Three weeks and still I'm
    Watching what you do

                  DAVID AND LEILA
What do I have to prove
to put my lovin' in the middle of your very
        next move?
Oh-my-God-oh-my-God-oh-my-God!

ROAR/SHAKE/ROAR/SHAKE.

DAVID

Oh my God!

David bolts to the doorway of his office simultaneously calling out.

DAVID

Leila! C'mon!

Leila struggles to a sitting position with a big smile on her face.

DAVID

Leila!

Leila looks over at David, smiling, and starts to rise.
BLACKOUT/ROAR/SHAKE/CRASH/SHAKE and we hear Leila's screams and David calling her name.
ROAR/CRASH/SHAKE/CRASH/SHAKE, silence.

DAVID

Leila?

LEILA

– – –

DAVID

Say something! Leila? Please!

LEILA

– – –

DAVID

Oh no! Oh my God! Oh no! Baby? Would you please
say something please?

Another aftershock: SHAKE/CRASH/SMASH, *silence.*
*David drops to the ground, searching for Leila. Over
and over he begs her to say anything! He stands up and
stumbles around the debris—the wreck of furniture and
broken walls and fallen ceiling. He finds a small candle
and he lights it and now he finds Leila and he drops to the
ground again taking her into his arms.*

DAVID

Help!

Crushed by the Rock I Been Standing On

(David's solo)

DAVID

(Spoken) This doesn't make any sense!

(Sung) You were laughing and smiling at me and
    romance!
And so sweet! I felt I had one more (magical) chance
just to hold you the way that I feel
real close real close whenever we could be together
And now I can't tell whether
you're breathing or not! You could be
dying
and I'm trying
I'm trying to pray
I'm trying but you could be dying
and why?

Who would hurt you like this?
How could it happen right here in the Church!
I'd give up my life for your kiss!

(I'm crushed)
I'm crushed by the rock I been standing on
(I'm crushed)
I'm crushed by the rock I been handing on
to anyone who'd listen to me in my search
for a way to deserve my everyday bliss!

Who would hurt you like this?
I'd give up my life for your kiss!
And I'm trying
I'm trying to pray
I'm trying but you could be dying
and why?

Mike and Tiffany in what's left of her apartment.

Duet in the Middle of Terrible Duress

(Mike and Tiffany)

MIKE

Is everything okay?

TIFFANY

Oh, everything is fine! And now
that you're here it's perfect somehow!
I've spent
the last forty-five minutes trying to figure out
this tent!
I can't find a flashlight
that works or a phone I can use
and who knows how I'm supposed to be handling
the news!
The radio's down and the neighbors bailed out like major
league jerks!
It's perfectly fine and completely all right
that the water's turned off for the rest of the night
or the week! No water! No windows!
And the closet collapsed on my clothes
and my camera! How did you get here!

MIKE

It took me a while! I was nowhere near
your side of town when it hit
The streets are cracked up pretty good
and packed
with people standing around in blankets! I should
probably bring you something like a first-aid kit!

TIFFANY

But why did you come?

MIKE

You know you're not at all
the same
as anyone I ever knew!
And it'd be dumb
And I'd be sorry
if I came up short or lame
where you're concerned I've wanted to
come through!

TIFFANY

(Then) Why can't we fly?
Is there some other woman? Is there a man?
A secret agenda?
An underground plan?

MIKE

No!
I feel this really great connection
with you!
A special bond!

TIFFANY

Special as in fond of nothing to be done and nothing to do?
But no desire as in physical fire?

MIKE

I like how we are
Riding around in the car!

TIFFANY

How long have I been waiting for a train
that never made it to the tracks!

MIKE

I thought we're friends!

TIFFANY

Maybe, Mike, maybe you're gay! Maybe you're queer!

MIKE

Me, queer!?

TIFFANY

Yes!
That's what I said!
It just came to me!
It just got through a really thick
part of my head!
Maybe you're queer! Maybe you're gay!

MIKE

Me? What should I say!
Maybe I'm queer?
Aw, No! I don't think so!
If you mean physically—

TIFFANY
Oh, I do mean physically—

MIKE
because I don't feel
the way that you want me to deal—

TIFFANY
I mean what you do or you don't feel
That's real
for you

MIKE
Maybe—Jesus Christ—maybe you're right!

TIFFANY
Obviously this is not a good night! And then again maybe
there's nothing the matter with me!
That sure would be an enormous relief
from a mess of crazy personal grief!

MIKE
So we're not breaking up!

TIFFANY
I do not exactly qualify
for partnership
with you!

MIKE
We're breaking up!

TIFFANY

It's broken! Let's just say we're
taking up
a new direction!

MIKE

Then it's okay between you and me?

TIFFANY

Okay? No! Nothing's okay!
But, you're all right!
You're just all wrong for me!
And now that's perfect somehow!
Because I can't find a flashlight
that works or a phone I can use
And who knows how I'm supposed to be handling
the news! No water! No windows!
Anything goes!

Rick, suddenly appearing.

RICK

Is everything okay?

*Mike and Tiffany, startled, and laughing, and Tiffany
throws herself into Rick's arms as she laughs.*

TIFFANY

Hey! What about lunch!

MIKE

Hey! What about me?

Consuelo and Dewain in what's left of Dewain's prison cell.

Dewain's Song of Liberation and Surprise

DEWAIN

I saw the moon in the morning
I felt the water on dry land
I saw the moon in the morning
I found the river in the sand

And the walls shook and they fell
And I heard the shattering
And I heard I felt the roar
of the devil climbing out of hell

And the air itself was battering
The windows! And the door
flew open and my books crashed to the floor
And it was like a miracle of fish
and flowers covering up the chaos of my cell

But I could not trust my feet
because the ground was weird and incomplete
So I stood still.
I said, "I am the way I will
be free.

It doesn't matter where/I put my head to bed:
I'm here!
I am the way I will
be free,"
I said.
So I stood still.

(I saw the moon in the morning
I felt the water on the dry land
I saw the moon in the morning
I found the river in the sand)

¡Este País!/This Country

(duet by Consuelo and Dewain)

CONSUELO

¡Este País!/This Country!
it doesn't want you
and it doesn't want me!

CONSUELO AND DEWAIN

I think that this land belongs to a gun
And we have no rights standing under the sun

DEWAIN

So the earth in her fury shakes under the sea
And breaks down the locks and buries the key!

CONSUELO AND DEWAIN

How do I get
a license to live here?
How do I ask
for permission to stay?
Where can I move in the world
without fear?
What is the price
and who do I pay?

CONSUELO

This Country!
It doesn't want you
and it doesn't want me!

DEWAIN

And everything real is illegal it seems
from homeless to hungry to living on dreams!

CONSUELO

Home means nobody else can close the door
I'm going home! I am not a beggar or a whore!
I'm going back to the FMLN
I want to become political again!
I want to keep the hope for land
and the open hand
of justice
alive inside El Salvador!
Dewain?
Will you come home with us!
Will you come home with me?
¡Ven nosotros!
¡Ven conmigo!

DEWAIN

But you could be killed there!

CONSUELO

And you could be killed here!

DEWAIN

I wouldn't be much good
to you or me
outside my neighborhood!

This is where I belong!
This is where I started out a lightweight
on the scales and this is where
I need to weigh in heavy
as I can
and strong!
I have to stay
and fight for you and me
my way!

                        CONSUELO

¡Pero nuestro amor
y la niña!
¡Tan perdida!
¡No hay que hacer!
¡Y eso no puedo—
*eso no puedo entender!**

                        DEWAIN

Please don't talk to me in Spanish!

                        CONSUELO

Okay! *¡En inglés!*
I think that this land belongs to a gun!
And we have no rights standing under the sun!

                        DEWAIN

So the earth in her fury shakes under the sea
And breaks down the locks and buries the key!
But I am the way I will
be free!

CONSUELO AND DEWAIN

This Country!
It doesn't want you
and it doesn't want me!

Dewain and Consuelo embrace.

*(But what about our love
and our baby!
So much lost!
And there is nothing to do!
And that I am not able—
that I am not able to understand!)

One Last Look
at the Angel in Your Eyes

One last look at the angel in your eyes
And then no regrets
the fact that we met still fills me
with surprise
And the fire of my wanting you—That fire
never dies!
But the days and the nights
do not care about love
And there is no shelter
when push comes to shove

One last look at the angel
at the angel
       in your eyes

ENSEMBLE

F inale

DAVID
(Still holding Leila, wounded and silent, in his arms)
Baby
I can't call an ambulance
and even if I could
that wouldn't do any good
because the freeway
is down
and no hospital
is working
anywhere in town

LEILA
(Remembering her blues song, with or without the words)
For days I been dreaming about changing the news
for days I been dreaming about changing the news
but sometimes the news ain' something you choose

Leila is joined by Tiffany and Consuelo, who carry the words as well as the music.

TIFFANY AND CONSUELO
For days I been dreaming about changing the news
for days I been dreaming about changing the news
but sometimes the news ain' something you choose

DAVID
(To Leila, who is lying in his arms)
Let me tell you the Gospel
According to This Girl
Like to make me
Lose my religion . . .
make me/make me/make me
make me beg and beg for mercy!

LEILA
Which little girl you
screaming for?

MIKE
Anything so we straighten things out and we
        keep things clear
So we all know (like) exactly who we are
and nobody's confused or demoralized or queer!

TIFFANY
I can't find a flashlight
that works or a phone I can use
and who knows how I'm supposed to be handling
the news!

DEWAIN
I got sunlight
through the window
I got sunlight

on my shoes
I got sunlight
on my blues
I got light all over me!

CONSUELO

And you *mi amor!* You gave me your lips
And you held me so close in the dark
That all of the violence fell into eclipse
And wasteland became like a wonderful park

TUTTI

And the earth began to Rumble and Roar
and buildings began to crumble and fall
and there was no house
    and there was no highway anymore

I was looking at the ceiling and then I saw the sky!
I was searching for a reasonable reason for my smile
I was finding what I want washed out completely in
    denial
I was looking at the ceiling and then I saw the sky!
I was looking at the ceiling and then I saw the sky!

Rick's Awkward Love Song #2

RICK

(Stepping forward to sing to the audience a last time, by himself)

I was thinking/actually
I wanted to/what
about love?
I wanted to/what
about last thing when
you close your/if
you think we could/I
would meet you there!/Well
Okay! I wanted to/Actually
I was thinking/what
about love?

Gabrielle M. Wright